THE
Queen
of Heaven
Disarmed

The Principality that Jezebel Answers to!

Pastor Mary Brown

Senior Pastor, Hebron Harvest Ministries,
Newmarket, Ontario, Canada
Regional Coordinator of
Christian International Churches of Ontario

PUBLISHED BY

www.jubilee-resources.com

Jubilee Resources N.Z., P.O. Box 36-044, Wellington 6330, New Zealand
Jubilee Resources Australia Ltd, P.O. Box 1412, Sunnybank Hills QLD 4109, Australia
Jubilee Resources Canada, 65 Cedar Pointe Drive, Ste 177, Barrie, Ont. L4N 9R3 Canada
Jubilee Resources USA, 24307 Magic Mountain Parkway, #261, Valencia CA 91355-1292 USA

or our Internet Web site bookshop at www.jubilee-resources.com

ISBN # 1877203-65-3

Unless otherwise stated, all Scripture quotations are taken from the New King James Version of the Bible.

The author may be contacted care of her ministry's office:
Hebron Harvest Ministries
1-1111 Davis Drive, Suite 180,
Newmarket, Ontario L3Y 7V1 Canada

Contents

The Queen of Heaven Disarmed

FOREWORD

Pastor Mary Brown has written some vital information for the saints. She is writing from much research, experience and some Holy Spirit enlightenment. The things she shares may be hard for some to grasp its significance. Natural mind thinking will not grasp the spiritual impact of these evil principalities and demonic spirits that seek to ill-effect mankind through any means possible. The new age concepts that all religions are good and on the same road to heaven is contrary to scriptural facts.

My advice is to seek the truth on these matters without being offended at the author for bringing these things to light. I know Mary Brown as her Bishop-overseer. I can assure the reader that her only purpose is to bring the reader the knowledge of the truth concerning the Queen of Heaven. To be pre-warned is to be pre-armed to overcome all. Do not become over reactive to objects. Not every object, picture or carving has a spirit attached to it.

We need to be led by the Holy Spirit and hear God's thoughts things about which we are not sure whether there is a connection between the natural object and the spirit world. If the real truth on this subject is fully understood it will set you free from becoming bound, oppressed or wrongly involved with anything that has a satanic connection.

I encourage the reader to read carefully and seek to receive the spirit and understanding the author is trying to impart. Please use wisdom and maturity in sharing these truths with others so that it will be in balance to be a blessing.
God bless you, Mary Brown, for having the burden and vision to make these things known to the Body of Christ. We know that a lack of understanding of these matters is what Satan uses to work subtly against mankind and especially church members. May this book bring freedom, blessing and more spiritual maturity to the Body of Christ.

Dr. Bill Hamon
Apostle, Bishop of Christian International Ministries Network
Author of: The Day of the Saints, Apostles,
                    Prophets and the Coming Moves of God;
                    Prophets and Personal Prophecy;
                    Prophets and the Prophetic Movement;
                    Prophet Pitfalls and Principles;
                    The Eternal Church;
                    Birthing God's Purpose;
                    Fulfilling Your Personal Prophecy;
                    Prophetic Destiny and the Apostolic Reformation

To my loving Saviour, Jesus Christ
without whom I would be lost forever

To the intercessors
who have borne with me,
praying for me
through all of the warfare
so faithfully,
and especially to
the intercessory leader,
Pastor Betty Voegelin.

CHAPTER 1

INTRODUCTION

Rev 17:3-6

3   So he carried me away in the Spirit into the wilderness. And I saw a woman sitting on a scarlet beast which was full of names of blasphemy, having seven heads and ten horns.

4   The woman was arrayed in purple and scarlet, and adorned with gold and precious stones and pearls, having in her hand a golden cup full of abominations and the filthiness of her fornication.

5   And on her forehead a name was written: MYSTERY, BABYLON THE GREAT, THE MOTHER OF HARLOTS AND OF THE ABOMINATIONS OF THE EARTH.

6   I saw the woman, drunk with the blood of the saints and with the blood of the martyrs of Jesus. And when I saw her, I marveled with great amazement.

The Queen of Heaven comes in many guises and is called by many names. Here, she is referred to as the Mother of Harlots and Babylon the Great. The worship of this spirit can be traced as far back as the destruction of the Tower of Babel, when she used the name Semiramis. She has been worshipped for thousands of years and is still worshipped today. She has used the names Diana, Isis, Astarte, Frigg, Madonna, Virgin of Guadalupe, Our Lady of Fatima, and many others.

This spirit has been responsible for the destruction of millions of saints. She is at the root of witchcraft, occult practices, sexual perversion, abortion, child abuse, corruption and compromise.

God hates this spirit. In a discussion with Jeremiah, God forbids the prophet to even pray for those who worship this spirit, and He indicates that if Jeremiah does pray for these worshippers, He will not listen.

Jeremiah 7:16-20

16   "Therefore do not pray for this people, nor lift up a cry or prayer for them,

nor make intercession to Me; for I will not hear you.

17 "Do you not see what they do in the cities of Judah and in the streets of Jerusalem?

18 "The children gather wood, the fathers kindle the fire, and the women knead dough, to make cakes for the queen of heaven; and they pour out drink offerings to other gods, that they may provoke Me to anger.

19 "Do they provoke Me to anger?" says the Lord. "Do they not provoke themselves, to the shame of their own faces?"

20 Therefore thus says the Lord God: "Behold, My anger and My fury will be poured out on this place - on man and on beast, on the trees of the field and on the fruit of the ground. And it will burn and not be quenched."

This book is about one of the most severe battles that the Church has ever, or will ever face. It is not my intention to glorify the enemy, but rather to glorify God and to reveal His strategy in the battle. Although the final victory over this spirit will not occur until Jesus Himself leads the armies of the Church Triumphant in the final battle, we have a responsibility now to declare war. The problem with this war is that we have not been fighting with a full revelation.

Many intercessors have come against the Queen of Heaven spirit. They have tried to tear it down. They have prayed against it, they have shaken their fists at it, and they have shouted at it. They have prayed in the Name of Jesus and taken their authority against it. Yet this spirit continues to affect our churches, our homes, our communities and our nations. Witchcraft covens still thrive. Our children are taught magic in their schools. Hopeless, dying people consult psychics and mediums for answers. Abortions continue taking place in our hospitals. Child pornography and prostitution thrives. Violence erupts in our schools. Churches still split. What is the answer?

The Word of God tells us that the people perish when there is a lack of understanding. We need to understand how this spirit got its foothold and we need to recognize the many disguises that it wears. What I will be discussing in these chapters is a revelation that God has given me concerning this vital area of spiritual warfare. Once we understand how this spirit operates, we will begin to recognize things that we must do to overcome. God has shown me a three-fold strategy.

First of all, God has shown me that in order to be overcomers, we need to come out of agreement with the Queen of Heaven. Without realizing it, many of God's people have been deceived by this spirit. We have actually walked in agreement with it, and in most cases, we have not recognized it. What we need to realize is that by being in agreement with the Queen of Heaven spirit, or partnering with it, we have worshipped it. Whatever, or whoever controls our lives is the god we worship. If Jesus controls our lives, then He is the One we worship. However, if the Queen of Heaven has any control in our lives, it is she who is worshipped. We need to recognize how we have partnered with this spirit and renounce it once and for all.

Secondly, we need to be true worshippers of the Most High God. Jesus said that the day was coming when true worshippers would worship Him in Spirit and in Truth.

John 4:21 Jesus declared, "Believe me, woman, a time is coming when you will worship the Father neither on this mountain nor in Jerusalem.

True worship is a Lordship issue. It is not only proclaiming the Lordship of Jesus, but living in agreement with Him to such a degree that He is in fact the One in control of our lives. If enough of God's people break covenant with the Queen of Heaven and live as true worshippers, then the grasp that this spirit has on our territory will be dramatically weakened.

Thirdly, the Lord has shown me that we need to be clothed in white linen. In Revelation 19 we read that when Jesus led the armies of Heaven against the Queen of Heaven, this army was clothed in resplendent white linen. This heavenly army was the Church Triumphant. White linen speaks of righteousness and holiness, and we cannot fight this spirit unless we are so clothed.

Rev 19:14

> The armies of heaven were following him, riding on white horses and dressed in fine linen, white and clean.

We shall begin by delving into the historic and present day manifestations of this spirit. We will end by following the strategy of warfare.

It is my prayer, that as you read this book, you will recognize and define ways in which you or your family may have come into agreement with the Queen of Heaven. It is my prayer that you will not only enter into true repentance and renounce this spirit, but that you will make Jesus Christ of Nazareth the One who is truly Lord of your life. I pray that you will seek Him for the clothing of resplendent white linen and follow through with the revelation in order to enter into highly effective warfare.

CHAPTER 2

THE ROOTS OF THE QUEEN OF HEAVEN

Rev 17:3-6

3   So he carried me away in the Spirit into the wilderness. And I saw a woman sitting on a scarlet beast which was full of names of blasphemy, having seven heads and ten horns.

4   The woman was arrayed in purple and scarlet, and adorned with gold and precious stones and pearls, having in her hand a golden cup full of abominations and the filthiness of her fornication.

5   And on her forehead a name was written: MYSTERY, BABYLON THE GREAT, THE MOTHER OF HARLOTS AND OF THE ABOMINATIONS OF THE EARTH.

6   I saw the woman, drunk with the blood of the saints and with the blood of the martyrs of Jesus. And when I saw her, I marveled with great amazement.

At the time of John's revelation, the physical city of Babylon no longer existed. It had been destroyed just as the Old Testament prophets had foretold. (Isaiah 13:19-22, Jeremiah 51,52). The Babylon of revelation is a spirit. The religious system that emanated from Babylon impacted every civilization of the world. Babylon was once a geographical location, but long after its physical destruction, the spirit of Babylon infiltrated the world. There are three realms that the spirit of Babylon has impacted. The first one is the spiritual realm, affecting the worship of God; the second one is the governmental realm, impacting governments and earthly kingdoms; and the third realm is commerce, affecting economic structures.

Our purpose in this chapter is to discover the roots of this spiritual entity.

Genesis 10

1   Now this is the genealogy of the sons of Noah: Shem, Ham, and Japheth. And sons were born to them after the flood.

6   And the sons of Ham were Cush and Mizraim and Put and Canaan.

7   The sons of Cush were Seba, Havilah, Sabtah, Raamah, and Sabtechah; and the sons of Raamah were Sheba and Dedan.

8   Cush begot Nimrod; he began to be a mighty one on the earth.

9   He was a mighty hunter before the Lord; therefore it is said, "Like Nimrod the mighty hunter before the Lord."

10   And the beginning of his kingdom was Babel, Erech, Accad, and Calneh, in the land of Shinar.

11   From that land he went to Assyria and built Nineveh, Rehoboth Ir, Calah,

12   and Resen between Nineveh and Calah (that is the principal city).

Genesis 11

1   Now the whole earth had one language and one speech.

2   And it came to pass, as they journeyed from the east, that they found a plain in the land of Shinar, and they dwelt there.

3   Then they said to one another, "Come, let us make bricks and bake them thoroughly." They had brick for stone, and they had asphalt for mortar.

4   And they said, "Come, let us build ourselves a city, and a tower whose top is in the heavens; let us make a name for ourselves, lest we be scattered abroad over the face of the whole earth."

5   But the Lord came down to see the city and the tower which the sons of men had built.

6   And the Lord said, "Indeed the people are one and they all have one language, and this is what they begin to do; now nothing that they propose to do will be withheld from them.

7   "Come, let Us go down and there confuse their language, that they may not understand one another's speech."

8   So the Lord scattered them abroad from there over the face of all the earth, and they ceased building the city.

9   Therefore its name is called Babel, because there the Lord confused the language of all the earth; and from there the Lord scattered them abroad over the face of all the earth.

Nimrod was the founder of the Babylonian system. The Word tells us that he was a "mighty hunter before the Lord" This statement is not saying that Nimrod was approved of by God. In fact, if you go back to the original

Hebrew writings you will discover that what is really being said is that Nimrod was full of rebellion before God. The Hebrew word for Nimrod is marad and it means "he rebelled". He was full of pride, and pride is always the beginning of disaster. It was because of pride that Lucifer attempted to elevate himself above God. In addition to his own rebellion, Lucifer got one third of the angels in heaven to rebel with him.

When the Word says that Nimrod was mighty before the Lord, it translates more like "he was mighty in rebellion against the Lord." Nimrod was an evil leader, who attempted to elevate himself in the same way as Lucifer before him, and like Lucifer, Nimrod wasn't satisfied to simply elevate himself, so he spawned rebellion in those who surrounded him.

Listen to what Josephus, a noted historian, says about Nimrod's rebellion:

"Now it was Nimrod who excited them to such an affront and contempt of God.... He also gradually changed the government into tyranny, seeing no other way of turning men from the fear of God.. the multitudes were very ready to follow the determination of Nimrod and they built a tower, neither sparing any pains, nor being in any degree negligent about the work: and, by reason of the multitude of hands employed in it, it grew very high. The place wherein they built the tower is now called Babylon"

The land that Nimrod lived in had been dominated by the Kenites. The language that was spoken by everyone at that time was Chaldean (an early form of the Phoenician language). Nimrod conquered seven cities and founded a Sumerian empire in Babel. After founding this empire in Babel, Erech, Akkad, and Calneh, he invaded Assyria and built Nineveh, Rehoboth-Ir, Calah and Resen. He then unified the people in numerous construction projects, the most prominent of which was the Tower of Babel.

Nimrod wasn't satisfied to be an earthly king. He turned the people's belief in a personal relationship with God into a warped religion that was based on Nimrod becoming a self proclaimed mediator between them and God. There is some historical indication that many people thought that Nimrod was the Saviour that had been prophesied back in the Garden of Eden. Nimrod built the tower as an affront to God.

Nimrod was married to a woman by the name of Semiramis. People believed that the life of Semiramis was foretold by the stars and that after her death she became the constellation called Virgo and reigned in the heavens as the Queen of Heaven.

After Nimrod died, Semiramis claimed that Nimrod had come back from the dead as the sun god and impregnated her. She bore a child and named it Tammuz and declared that Tammuz was Nimrod reincarnated. Tammuz was symbolized by the golden calf. Nimrod, the sun god, was symbolized by fire, and later known as Baal. Nimrod was also symbolized by sun images, fish, trees, pillars, and animals.

Semiramis claimed that she had given birth to a saviour. However, she made sure that she became the object of worship and not Tammuz. She was worshipped as the mother of the son of god. She became the self proclaimed mother of all gods.

This Queen of Heaven story was told in every civilization. It was told in different names, but the story line was always the same. There was a form of Baal and a mother of gods who was called Astarte, Semiramis, and Innana, Venus, Diana or some other name.

God was grieved.

Romans 1:21-26

21 because, although they knew God, they did not glorify Him as God, nor were thankful, but became futile in their thoughts, and their foolish hearts were darkened.

22 Professing to be wise, they became fools,

23 and changed the glory of the incorruptible God into an image made like corruptible man and birds and four-footed animals and creeping things.

24 Therefore God also gave them up to uncleanness, in the lusts of their hearts, to dishonor their bodies among themselves,

25 who exchanged the truth of God for the lie, and worshiped and served the creature rather than the Creator, who is blessed forever. Amen.

26 For this reason God gave them up to vile passions.

This principality called the Queen of Heaven was named by God to be the Mother of Harlots, or the Harlot of Babylon.

Revelation 17:5

5 And on her forehead a name was written: MYSTERY, BABYLON THE GREAT, THE MOTHER OF HARLOTS AND OF THE ABOMINATIONS OF THE EARTH.

On thing that we must always keep in mind when discussing the spiritual realm is that spirits are not people. They use people, and work through people, but it is not people who are the enemy. The Queen of Heaven is a principality, not a person.

Ephesians 6:12

12   For we do not wrestle against flesh and blood, but against principalities, against powers, against the rulers of the darkness of this age, against spiritual hosts of wickedness in the heavenly places.

This is the beginning of goddess worship in history. In the next chapters, we will examine some of the manifestations of the Queen of Heaven throughout history and in the world we live in today.

CHAPTER 3

Ishtar

Ishtar was another manifestation of the worship of the Queen of Heaven on planet earth. This goddess was also known as Innana, Innin, Astarte, Ashtar, Aphrodite, Venus, Lady of the Battle, and in Israel, the Queen of Heaven. It is this goddess that the people of Israel were often guilty of worshipping, and for which they went into captivity. Ashteroth, is another name for Astarte, and is formed by combining the consonants from Astarte and the vowels from the Hebrew word "boshet", which means shame. It was shame indeed that the Israelites heaped on their heads by going after this goddess. Today's goddess worshippers call her Venus, the goddess of love.

This is the story of Ishtar that her worshippers believe:

Ishtar was not satisfied with the title "Queen of Heaven" which she had usurped from former Sumerian goddesses. She also wanted to be known as the Queen of the Netherworld. This title was supposedly held by Ishtar's sister Ereshkigal. When Ishtar descended into the Netherworld she had to pass through seven gates. At each of the gates she was stripped of one of her garments. At the first gate she had her crown removed. At the second gate, her earrings, at the third gate, her necklace, at the fourth gate, her breast ornaments, at the fifth gate, her girdle, at the sixth gate, her bracelets, and finally, at the seventh gate, her cloak. When she went through the final gate, Ereshkigal killed her and put her corpse on a stake. Ishtar was then resurrected by the other gods on the condition that a substitute for her be found. She chose as her substitute her husband Tammuz, who was the supposed son of Semiramis.

This goddess became so influential in various civilizations of the world, that she was known as the most powerful goddess of all times. Would be kings believed that if they slept with her, they would receive their kingships. It is on record that Sargon was one of them.

Sargon ruled the whole Euphrates valley around 3800 B.C. and was the founder of a Semitic dominion over the region of Sumer and built the city of

Akkad. He conquered many lands and proclaimed himself to be "King over the four corners of the earth." Sargon was not a mythical figure, but a real king. There is much evidence to support the fact that he was a worshipper of Ishtar. *(From THE STORY GREATEST NATIONS AND THE WORLD'S FAMOUS EVENTS, Volume 1, a historical reference book first published in 1813 by Edward S. Ellis and Charles F. Horne, PhD.)*

There are many rituals associated with Ishtar. The first one is a ritual that was held to commemorate the death of Tammuz. It was held to appease Ishtar's grief over his loss. This ritual took on the form of a fast and it was called the "fast of lamentation". In some temples, the ritual also involved shaving the head as a sign of mourning. Anyone who refused was bound to prostitute themselves to strangers and sacrifice to the goddess the wages of their shame.

The second ritual was performed by a king or high ranking official of the day. He was said to represent Tammuz. The king would have a marriage ceremony with Ishtar's high priestess which took place on New Year's Day.

The third ritual was a celebration of Ishtar's menstrual cycle. It took place at the time of the full moon and was celebrated with a day of rest. Interestingly enough it was called "Sabattu". The devil is always trying to counterfeit what belongs to God.

Another ritual was performed on the first Sunday of the spring season. The families rose early in the morning and stood facing the east to await the rising of the sun. As the sun came up they would give worship to the sun god, Baal, by bowing down to him in various postures. (Many of these postures are used today in Yoga.) After those rituals were performed, the children would invoke the goddess to help them and they would go on an egg hunt. The eggs were thought to have come from rabbits, which were the symbol of lust, sexual prowess, and reproduction. It was believed that the rabbit had once actually been a bird that Ishtar changed magically into a four footed animal, hence its ability to lay eggs. The eggs were symbols of fertility, sex and new life.

There were many other rituals, some of them still being practiced in other forms today. The rituals usually involved music, ritual prostitution, cross dressing, and perversions of all kinds. In societies that embraced the worship of this goddess, every young girl had to serve as a temple prostitute for a season before she could be given in marriage. Some women were also forced to leave their husbands for seasons to serve as prostitutes in the temples. The money received for the prostitution was donated to the goddess.

In some temples, young boys also had to prostitute themselves to men who preferred young boys to young girls. Homosexuality was freely accepted in these societies.

Notice, that some of these rituals, particularly the hunt for eggs laid by a rabbit, are used today in celebration of Easter (Ishtar). Easter revolves around pagan rituals and should never have been associated with the resurrection of Jesus. This celebration infiltrated the early Roman Catholic Church and was a compromise used to keep those who wanted these celebrations from leaving the Church.

I much prefer to use the term, "Resurrection Day"!

It was this goddess that Jezebel worshipped. We will discuss Jezebel in another chapter and in the chapter concerning compromise we will examine the worship of this entity by Israel. We will learn just what the worship of this spirit cost Israel in terms of their relationship with God.

CHAPTER 4

Diana of Ephesus (Artemis)

Diana of Ephesus figured prominently in the world of Paul's day. Paul himself had an encounter with followers of this goddess. The account is found in Acts 19:23-41.

23 And during that time, there was some serious trouble in Ephesus about the Way of Jesus.

24 A man named Demetrius, who worked with silver, made little silver models that looked like the temple of the goddess Artemis. Those who did this work made much money.

25 Demetrius had a meeting with them and some others who did the same kind of work. He told them, "Men, you know that we make a lot of money from our business.

26 But look at what this man Paul is doing. He has convinced and turned away many people in Ephesus and in almost all of Asia! He says the gods made by human hands are not real.

27 There is a danger that our business will lose its good name, but there is also another danger: People will begin to think that the temple of the great goddess Artemis is not important. Her greatness will be destroyed, and Artemis is the goddess that everyone in Asia and the whole world worships."

28 When the others heard this, they became very angry and shouted, "Artemis, the goddess of Ephesus, is great!"

29 The whole city became confused. The people grabbed Gaius and Aristarchus, who were from Macedonia and were traveling with Paul, and ran to the theater.

30 Paul wanted to go in and talk to the crowd, but the followers did not let him.

31 Also, some leaders of Asia who were friends of Paul sent him a message, begging him not to go into the theater.

32 Some people were shouting one thing, and some were shouting another. The meeting was completely confused; most of them did not know why they had come together.

33 The Jews put a man named Alexander in front of the people, and some of them told him what to do. Alexander waved his hand so he could explain things to the people.

34 But when they saw that Alexander was a Jew, they all shouted the same thing for two hours: "Great is Artemis of Ephesus!"

35 Then the city clerk made the crowd be quiet. He said, "People of Ephesus, everyone knows that Ephesus is the city that keeps the temple of the great goddess Artemis and her holy stone that fell from heaven.

36 Since no one can say this is not true, you should be quiet. Stop and think before you do anything.

37 You brought these men here, but they have not said anything evil against our goddess or stolen anything from her temple.

38 If Demetrius and those who work with him have a charge against anyone they should go to the courts and judges where they can argue with each other.

39 If there is something else you want to talk about, it can be decided at the regular town meeting of the people.

40 I say this because some people might see this trouble today and say that we are rioting. We could not explain this, because there is no real reason for this meeting."

41 After the city clerk said these things, he told the people to go home.

When Paul was preaching the gospel in Ephesus, such revival broke out that the people of the town destroyed their idols and turned to Christ in great numbers. This affected the economy of the whole area. Ephesus was wealthy, due in part to the tourist trade of pilgrims coming to worship at the temple of Diana, and due in part to the money the local artisans received for their renderings of Diana's image.

The beliefs concerning Diana were very much like the beliefs concerning Nimrod and Semiramis. Diana was believed to be the twin sister of Apollo and the daughter of Zeus. She was also known as Isis or Artemis, depending on which location the worshippers were living in. It was believed that she had a divine son named Horus.

She was sometimes called the moon goddess.

Diana was considered to be a great hunter. It was often said that she was more at home among the animals than she was among humans. She didn't like humans very well, especially men. It was rumored that she would kill anyone who came too close to her. She was not exactly known for her mercy either, since it was reported that she would kill anyone who offended her.

Diana was also known as the goddess of fertility of wood and glade. She was believed to be the goddess of chastity, and she was called upon by women at their times of childbirth in hopes that she would magically ease their pain. To followers of Diana, chastity did not mean that they never had sex. It meant that they were not in a committed relationship.

For over a thousand years this goddess with her temple was a focal point for the religious, economic, and cultural life of her worshippers.

Diana is still worshipped today. Many modern witches' covens have given her the title Diana Lucifer, the mistress of all elements. There is a legend in witchcraft concerning Diana. It was said that Diana divided herself to create darkness and light, and that the light is Lucifer. She then used magic to charm and seduce Lucifer. She traded places with a cat to fool him. The offspring of Lucifer and Diana was called Aradia and she was proclaimed Queen of the Witches. Diana taught Aradia witchcraft and instructed her to teach this "craft" to mortals on the earth.

There were several believed manifestations of Aradia.

She was believed to have manifested herself as Herodias in the Bible. (the one responsible for beheading John the Baptist. Mark 6)

Aradia manifested herself as a female Christ figure in 14th century Italy and taught witchcraft. She taught at a place called Nemi. The site was excavated in 1885 by Sir John Savile Lumley who was the English ambassador to Rome. The site was called Artemisium Nemorense and became a place of worship to Diana Luciana as well as a hydro therapeutic establishment. A man by the name of Orestes was supposed to have murdered the king of Troas here and as a result of claiming the land as his own he instituted Diana worship at this place. When Orestes died, the worshippers took his bones and buried them in front of the temple to Saturn. The ritual that ensued on this spot was one of human sacrifice. Fire was used as part of the ritual. For a season, any stranger who accidentally ventured onto this site was sacrificed on the altar of Diana. During the diggings, it was verified that on the northern shore of the Lake on which the modern town Nemi is perched, there was a sacred grove and sanctuary of Diana Nemorensis, or Diana of the Wood. Tests have substantiated the claim that this particular grove had indeed been used for worship and rituals dating as far back as 495 BC. Remains of human sacrifices were found.

Concerning Aradia, Leland, in his book, entitled, "Aradia: Gospel of Witches", writes: "she traveled far and wide, teaching and preaching the religion of the old times, the religion of Diana, the Queen of the Fairies and of the Moon, the goddess of the poor and the oppressed. And the fame of her wisdom and beauty went forth over all the land, and people worshipped her, calling her La Bella Pellegrina (the beautiful pilgrim)".

In Siver RavenWolf's book, "To Ride a Silver Broomstick", it is said that Aradia was an Italian goddess sworn to protect her people against the aggression of masculine faith and its persecutors during the reign of medieval terror. Raven also says that the symbol of Aradia is the red garter.

In the book, "The Gods of Greece" by Stassinopoulos, Arianna and Roloff Beny, we read the following quote concerning Diana's aloofness and the effect of this goddess on people today: "When we experience the pull to privacy, the pull to be alone as an instinctual, animal need, it is Artemis (Diana) who is working through us. And when this pull becomes destructive, a chill lack of feeling that cuts us off from any real human communication, it is Artemis's (Diana's) darkness that is showing through."

In the next chapters we will continue by examining some of the expressions of goddess worship today.

CHAPTER 5

Paganism, Neo Paganism, Wicca, Witchcraft

A Definition of Paganism

In simplest terms Paganism is defined in the dictionary as a religion of place, or a native religion. The Native American's religion is called Pagan. Hinduism is also considered to be a form of Paganism.

One well known form of paganism is Druidism. Druidism is a form of paganism that developed among the ancient Celts. Druids were usually among the upper class of Celtic society and worshipped many gods which were similar to the gods of the Greeks and Romans. All of their gods and goddesses were connected with nature. They were said to have magical powers which revolved around nature. They forecast events by interpreting the flight of birds and by reading the markings on the livers and entrails of animals which they believed were sacred. They were known for having most of their worship rituals out of doors in sacred groves and woodlands. Modern druids have tried to study and maintain the ancient rituals.

Another form of paganism is witchcraft, although many pagans would say that witchcraft is the occult form of paganism. The beliefs, however, are very closely related. Witchcraft, like Druidism, is centered around the worship of the goddess and the worship of nature. Some witches also recognize various male forms of gods, but the emphasis is more on the female. The politically correct name for modern witchcraft is Wicca. Wicca itself has absorbed elements of other systems such as the Qabala and elements of Hindu.

Other forms of paganism are Hinduism, Shamanism, Voodoo, the Fetish religion, from which Voodoo was derived, and various native religions from around the world.

Modern paganism, or neo-paganism, has the following characteristics:

Pagans believe in many gods and goddesses with a greater emphasis on the goddess. They believe that the earth is the mother goddess, female in nature, hence the term "mother nature", or "mother earth". Another name commonly used is "Gaia". She is believed to be the creatrix of the entire physical realm. Pagans believe that because mother earth is creatrix, all creatures are siblings of man.

Pagans live their lives around the cycles of nature. They believe that each of the four elements, fire, water, earth and air, can be controlled by magic and that you can become one with them. They believe that the four elements guard the god and goddess as well as themselves and that these elements, or "elementals" as they are sometimes called, guard the gateways between the natural realm and the spiritual realm. Some pagans actually have rituals for becoming one with each of these elements and for bringing them under their control.

Pagans do not believe in heaven or hell, but they embrace a belief in reincarnation.

Pagans believe that magic is the existence of energy that can be manipulated

Pagans worship the goddess in three forms: (maiden, mother and crone)

Independence is to be sought after and attained

WHEEL OF THE YEAR

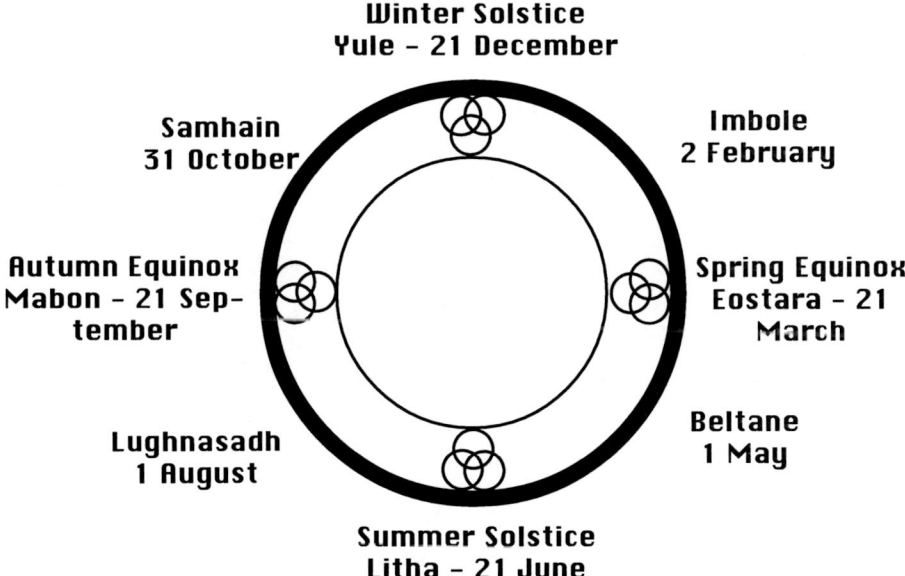

Winter Solstice
Yule – 21 December

Samhain
31 October

Imbole
2 February

Autumn Equinox
Mabon – 21 Sep-
tember

Spring Equinox
Eostara – 21
March

Lughnasadh
1 August

Beltane
1 May

Summer Solstice
Litha – 21 June

For the pagan worshipper, the wheel of the year represents the journey of the sun across the sky. Since goddess worship is all tied up with the worship of the sun, this makes sense. It is all about solstices, equinoxes and the Earth's changing seasons. Each spoke of the wheel marks a moment of progression and change in the Earth. They celebrate the holiday starting the day before until the day after the Sabbat date.

The pagan religious calendar contains 13 Full Moon celebrations and 8 Sabbats or days of power. The Sabbats are solar rituals, marking the points of the Sun's yearly cycle, and are but half of the ritual year. The Esbats are the Full Moon celebrations. There are 12-13 Full Moons yearly, or one every 28 1/4 days.

The Moon is a symbol of the Goddess as well as a source of energy. Thus, after the religious aspects of the Esbats, they often practice magic, tapping into the larger amounts of energy which they believe exists at these times. Most rites are held at night. The eight Sabbats represent seasonal birth, death, and rebirth to the pagan worshipper. Some of the rituals performed at this time are peculiar to wicca and witchcraft.

The following are the spokes on the wheel of the year:

Yule/Winter Solstice

From December 21st through December 31st.

The shortest day of the year and the longest night.

The goddess gives birth to a son, the god.

It is celebrated by fire and the use of the Yule log. A portion of the Yule log is saved to be used in lighting next Year's log. (Usually oak.) This piece is kept throughout the year to protect the home. The Yule log is burned to give life and power to the Sun.

Bayberry candles are also burned to ensure wealth and happiness throughout the following year.

The reindeer stag is also a reminder of the horned god.

Traditional Pagan foods are roasted turkey, nuts, eggnog and mulled wine.

Incense is made from bayberry, cedar, pine and rosemary.

Candles are gold, red, green and white.

Sacred Gemstones used in rituals are cat's eye and ruby.

Candlemas/Imbolc

February 2nd.

Marks the time to welcome spring.

The recovery of the goddess after giving birth to the god.

This celebration is considered to be a festival of light and of fertility.

Self-dedication rituals are performed or renewed.

The celebration represents new beginnings and spiritual growth, and the "sweeping out of the old." (It is from here that we get the expression, "A new broom sweeps clean".

Foods eaten at this celebration are sunflower seeds, poppyseed breads and cakes and herbal Teas.

Incense is made from basil, myrrh and wisteria

Candles used in rituals are brown, pink and red.

Gemstones used in rituals are amethyst, garnet, onyx and turquoise.

Ostara/Spring Equinox

March 21st.

Marks the 1st day of true spring.

The pagan believes that this is the time when the goddess blankets the earth with fertility, bursting forth from her sleep, as the god stretches and grows to maturity. He walks the greening fields and delights in the abundance of Nature.

This is a time of beginnings, of action, of planting spells for future gains, and of tending ritual gardens.

Eggs are colored and placed on the altar as talismans. The familiar Easter Bunny is a Pagan derivative, as are baskets of flowers.

The colors light green, lemon yellow and pale pink are traditional for this holiday.

Foods eaten at this celebration are hard boiled eggs, honey cakes and the 1st fruits of the season.

Incense is made from the african violet, jasmine, rose, sage and strawberry.

Candles used in rituals are gold, green, yellow.

Gemstones used in rituals are amethyst, aquamarine, bloodstone and red jasper.

Beltane/Mayday

May 1st.

This is a celebration of what the pagan believes to be the union of the goddess and god, and thus is also a fertility festival.

It is also a celebration of the returning sun (or sun god).

The traditional colors for Mayday are red and white.

Flower petals are strewn about the circle and later swept into a pole and distributed around the perimeter of the house for protection.

Foods eaten are red fruits, herbal salads, red or pink wine punch, and large, round oatmeal or barley cakes.

Incense is made from frankincense, lilac and rose.

Candles used in rituals are dark green in color.

Gemstones used in rituals are emerald, orange carnelian, sapphire and rose quartz.

Summer Solstice/Midsummer

June 21st.

Marks the longest day of the year.

Midsummer is a classic time for pagans to perform magic of all kinds. Pagans believe that whatever they dream of on this night will come true for the dreamer.

It is considered to be a celebration of passion and success.

Foods eaten are fresh vegetables, summer fruits, pumpernickel bread, ale and mead.

Incense is made from frankincense, lemon, myrrh, pine, rose and wisteria.

Candles used for rituals are blue, green, gold and red.

Gemstones used in rituals are all green stones (emerald and jade).

Lammas/Lughnasadh

August 2nd.

The time of the first harvest

The pagans believe that this is the time when the god loses his strength as the sun rises farther in the South each day and the nights grow longer. The god is thought to be dying, and yet it is believed that the god lives on inside the goddess as her child. (This goes right back to Semiramis and Nimrod).

Foods eaten at this time are homemade breads (wheat, oat and corn bread), nuts, wild berries, apples, rice, berry pies, elderberry wine, ale and meadowsweet tea.

Incense is made from aloes, rose, and sandlewood.

Candles used in rituals are orange and yellow.

Gemstones used in rituals are aventurine, citrine, peridot, and sardonyx.

Autumn Equinox/Mabon

September 21st.

For this pagan, this day marks the completion of the harvest. Day and Night are equal. The god prepares to leave his physical body toward renewal and rebirth of the goddess.

It is considered to be a time for meditation.

River and stream stones gathered over the summer have rituals and incantations done over them so that they can be empowered for various purposes.

Foods eaten are corn bread cakes, wheat products, breads, nuts, vegetables, apples, cider, carrots, onions, potatoes and pomegranates.

Incense is made from benzoin, myrrh and sage.

Candles used in rituals are brown, green, orange, yellow.

Gemstones used in rituals are carnelian, lapis lazuli, sapphire, and yellow agate.

Halloween/Samhain "sow-en"

October 31st

This is a celebration to say farewell to the god.

It is considered to be a temporary farewell. He isn't wrapped in eternal darkness but the pagan believes that he will be reborn through the goddess at Yule.

It is said to be the time when the veil between the worlds is very thin, when souls that are leaving this physical plane can pass out and souls that are reincarnating can pass in.

This holiday is considered the Witches' New Year, representing one full turn of the seasonal year. It is a time of reflection, of looking back over the last year and honoring ancestors and all those who have gone before.

It is said that lighting a new orange-colored candle at midnight on Samhain and allowing it to burn until sunrise will bring one good luck; however, bad luck will befall those who bake bread on this day or journey after sunset.

The reason for the costumes worn on this day is that the pagan believes that on this night, when the veil between the worlds is thin and souls are moving about between the worlds they could be frightened by people doing rituals in grave yards. The worshippers disguise themselves in costumes so that the dead souls will think the living are really dead. Wearing a costume is associated with being dead.

Black candles are used to ward off negativity.

Wiccan traditions that are performed at this time are runecasting, making Jack-o-lanterns and standing before a mirror and making a secret wish.

Foods eaten are apples, pumpkin pie, hazelnuts, corn, cranberry muffins and breads, ale, cider and herbal teas.

Incense is made from apple, heliotrope, mint, nutmeg and sage.

Candles used in rituals are black and orange

Gemstones used in rituals are all black and include jet, obsidian and onyx.

Do you recognize any of the celebrations? Some of the things that we thought were just innocent fun aren't. Without even realizing it, we have incorporated rituals used in goddess worship into our celebrations of the birth of Christ and the resurrection of Christ, not to mention our Thanksgiving celebrations.

If you have been involved in any pagan religion, including witchcraft, my advice is to run, not walk, to get ministry. I am including some prayers here that can be prayed for the purposes of renouncing the worship of the goddess.

"I believe that Jesus Christ was born of a virgin. I believe that He lived on earth fully God and fully man. I believe that He lived a sinless life and was obedient to the Father at all times. I believe that He was crucified in the flesh as a sacrifice for my sins and diseases, and that He rose again on the third day, triumphant over hell, death and the grave. I believe that He ascended into heaven and is seated at the right hand of the Father to make intercession for the saints. I believe that He will return again to reign upon the earth with His bride. It is this Jesus that I declare to be my Lord and Saviour.

I renounce, now and forever, every covenant and agreement that I or my ancestors have made with the Queen of Heaven. I renounce and repent for every behaviour, known or unknown, that has given this spirit any right in my life. I renounce and repent for any way in which I or my ancestors have entered into rebellion against God.

I renounce every name of the Queen of Heaven. I renounce Semerimas, Queen of Heaven, Mother of Harlots, the Harlot of Babylon, Jezebel, Ishtar, Innan, Innin, Astarte, Ashtar, Aphrodite, Venus, Lady of the Battle, Erishkigal, Diana, Artemis, Herodias, Aradia, La Bella Pellegrina, the goddess of the Hunt, goddess of chastity, Baalith, Belith, Athene, Ashteroth, Mother Earth, Black Madonna, Mother Nature, Goddess Mother, Neith, Angerona, Aurora, Goddess of the Dawn, Bellona, Cardea, Flora, Juterna, Juventas, Latona, Goddess of Light, Libitina, Mefitis, Minerva, Slacia, Vesta, Frigg, and any other names used for the Queen of Heaven.

I renounce and repent for any ways that I or my ancestors may have entered into the worship of the sun.

I renounce and repent for any ways in which I or my ancestors have compromised our obedience to God's commands.

I renounce and repent for any way in which I or my ancestors may have become involved with the occult.

I renounce the reading of tea leaves, the pendulum, ouija boards, horoscopes, water witching, Psychic readings, voodoo, witchcraft, enchantments, good luck charms, superstition of all kinds, reading of entrails, tarot cards, seances, necromancy, spiritism, hexes, vexes, spells, divinations, incantations, sorcery, or any other form of occult practice.

I renounce all manipulation of the spirit realm through talismans, rituals and incantations.

I renounce all attempts to become one with the elements.

I renounce all astral projection.

I renounce the wheel of the year, and celebrations surrounding the sun, moon, or stars.

I renounce Yule and winter solstice celebrations, including the burning with fire of the Yule log for purposes of protection. I confess that God is my protector.

I renounce the burning of bayberry candles for the purposes of ensuring good luck and wealth. I confess that God is my provider.

I renounce the horned god.

I renounce the Candlemas or Imbolic festivals. I renounce all making of cakes for the Queen of Heaven. I renounce and break off of my life all dedication rituals to the Queen of Heaven in any form. I dedicate my life to the One true God through the shed Blood of Jesus Christ of Nazareth.

I renounce all Ostara spring rituals. I renounce the using of eggs for talismans. I renounce the planting of spells for future gain and the tending of ritual gardens.

I specifically renounce Astarte and all pagan celebrations surrounding her.

I renounce all celebrations of Beltane, and dancing around the May pole. I renounce all fertility rituals and confess that God is the giver of Life.

I renounce the placement of flower petals around my house for protection and proclaim Jesus to be my protector.

I renounce all celebrations of the summer solstice. I renounce the magic spells done in this season. I renounce divination and all practices of worship to the goddess. I renounce all rituals of sacrifice and fertility.

I renounce the celebration of Lammas and proclaim that God is not dying but is alive. I repent for the offering up of sacrifices in rituals to celebrate the death of god.

I renounce Mabon and all meditation done in celebration of this date. I renounce all forms of meditation that lead to astral projection. I renounce the use of crystals and gemstones for purposes of personal empowerment.

I renounce all celebrations of Samhain or Hallowe'en. I renounce all attempts to communicate with the dead. I renounce veneration of ancestors. I renounce the burning of the Jack O Lantern for bringing good luck. I renounce the casting of Runes. I renounce making secret wishes before a mirror. I renounce the wearing of costumes to associate with death.

I renounce all desire to gain power and control over the elements, over the spirit realm, and over other people. I renounce control in all forms. I renounce all worship of nature. I renounce Mother Earth.

I renounce every pagan practice, and I ask you to forgive me. Wash me in the Blood of Jesus and cleanse me from all unrighteousness. I thank you Jesus, for Your love for me.

Let us continue looking at modern manifestations of goddess worship in our society today.

CHAPTER 6

FEMINISM

Many women in the feminist movement are involved in goddess worship, although we rarely hear about it. The agenda of goddess worship has been well hidden while feminists have attempted to gain control in the arenas of politics and economics. Only now that they have begun to make inroads in these areas is the whole agenda coming out of the closet.

Here is a quotation from a book entitled Changing of the Gods by Naomi Goldenberg:

"The feminist movement in Western culture is engaged in the slow execution of Christ and Yahweh. It is likely that as we watch Christ and Yahweh tumble to the ground, we will completely outgrow the need for an external God."

The feminist worships the goddess because they believe that the goddess is really them. They see themselves as divine. They see their bodies as sacred, and they see aggression as a healthy thing. They believe that anger purifies them. What it all boils down to is out and out rebellion and in the guise of personal rights.

Listen to this quote from a witch who works with a Catholic priest at the Institute of Creation Spirituality"

"We are already one with the goddess. She has been with us from the beginning, so fulfillment becomes. A matter of self awareness. For women, the goddess is the symbol of the inmost self. She awakens the mind and spirit and emotions."

One thing that is really disturbing is that this whole agenda has somehow infiltrated the more liberal denominations of the Christian church. A Christian feminist by the name of Mary Daly says this about traditional Christianity: "to put it bluntly, I propose that Christianity itself should be castrated."

At the Perkins School of Theology at the Southern Methodist University they hold seminars on women's studies. One such seminar is called "Wisdom Weaving" and it teaches goddess worship, metaphysics, and Spiritism. One of the speakers for that course is Linda Finnell, a wiccan witch. She teaches a class called, "Returning to the Goddess Through Dianic Witchcraft."

Many liberal churches in North America hire individuals who hold a metaphysical world view.

This feminism is merely a further development of ancient goddess worship. It paves the way in our society for the following:

• Acceptance of Witchcraft

• The teaching of witchcraft in our schools

• Promoting movies like Harry Potter (there has actually been a school opened in New York for children to apprentice in witchcraft because of the popularity of the book)

• Legalizing abortions

• Experimenting with cloning and other reproductive methods including invitro fertilization. It is all with the purpose in mind of doing away with the need of males in our society and make it possible for self reproduction Please understand that I am not saying that anyone who has had to have medical intervention to get pregnant is in agreement with the Queen of Heaven. However, we need to recognize why some of these medical procedures were researched in the first place. The radical feminist truly wants to do away with any need of the male partner for reproduction.

• Acceptance of homosexuality as a norm in our society

• Taking prayer out of the schools

• Banning the reading of Scripture in schools

• Young offenders act

• Sunday night sex show that teaches children every form of sexual perversion

The feminist movement has also been responsible for a great deal of the ecological movement. While we have been given the responsibility by God to care for the earth, we have never been instructed to worship it.

Some feminists believe that the patriarchal system that they are fighting dominates both animals and women. They see themselves in the same category as animals in society and so they believe that by fighting for animal rights they are fighting for their own rights. However, they take this fight to the extreme. Many feminists also refuse to eat meat of any kind because they see the animals equal with themselves.

I am not saying in this chapter that we should not love animals. I am not condemning those who have pets that they love. I myself have three beautiful cats that I enjoy immensely. However, the feminist agenda is not really a true love of animals. It is all about their struggle to be free from the domination of men. It is not simply an appreciation for what God has created.

We must also understand what it is that has given the feminist movement an open door into our society. It goes right back to the Garden of Eden and the plot which Satan had to exalt himself. One part of his strategy has been to warp the godly relationship that was intended between men and women. Women were created to stand beside man as a helpmeet. They were intended to be a team and the man was intended to be the one responsible for the health of that team. It is not the fault of all men, just as it is not the fault of all women. It is a strategy of Satan. Period!

If you have ever been a part of the feminist movement, or if you have been a supporter of it, the following prayer will be helpful to you.

"I believe that Jesus Christ was born of a virgin. I believe that He lived on earth fully God and fully man. I believe that He lived a sinless life and was obedient to the Father at all times. I believe that He was crucified in the flesh as a sacrifice for my sins and diseases, and that He rose again on the third day, triumphant over hell, death and the grave. I believe that He ascended into heaven and is seated at the right hand of the Father to make intercession for the saints. I believe that He will return again to reign upon the earth with His bride. It is this Jesus that I declare to be my Lord and Saviour.

I renounce, now and forever, every covenant and agreement that I or my ancestors have made with the Queen of Heaven. I renounce and repent for every behaviour, known or unknown, that has given this spirit any right in my life. I renounce and repent for any way in which I or my ancestors have entered into rebellion against God.

I renounce every name of the Queen of Heaven. I renounce Semerimas, Queen of Heaven, Mother of Harlots, the Harlot of Babylon, Jezebel, Ishtar, Innan, Innin, Astarte, Ashtar, Aphrodite, Venus, Lady of the Battle, Erishkigal, Diana, Artemis, Herodias, Aradia, La Bella Pellegrina, the goddess of the Hunt, goddess of chastity, Baalith, Belith, Athene, Ashteroth, Mother Earth, Black Madonna, Mother Nature, Goddess Mother, Neith, Angerona, Aurora, Goddess of the Dawn, Bellona, Cardea, Flora, Juterna, Juventas, Latona, Goddess of Light, Libitina, Mefitis,

Minerva, Slacia, Vesta, Frigg, and any other names used for the Queen of Heaven.

I renounce and repent for any ways that I or may ancestors may have entered into the worship of the sun.

I repent for all hatred of the opposite sex. I choose to forgive those who have hurt me. (Be specific here and put in the names of those who have hurt you and made you feel belittled)

I repent for any way in which I allowed my fear and pain to cause hurt to others. (Once again, be specific)

I repent for worship of animals and for equating myself with them.

I repent for any ways in which I have tried to make myself so independent that I would have no need for others, especially those of the opposite sex.

I confess that I am dependant on God.

I repent for the sin of rebellion and I submit myself to God.

I repent for any way in which I have agreed with or aided in removing prayer and the reading of God's Word from schools, even if the only way that I aided was in keeping silent.

I repent for any way in which I have agreed with or aided in the legalizing of abortion. (Those who have had abortions should also repent for that and in all cases should seek out counseling ministry for healing).

I repent for any way in which I have entered into sexual perversion. I repent for any way in which I have agreed with or aided in the promotion of pornography, homosexuality, and perversion of all kinds.

I repent for all involvement in the occult. (pray the prayer in Chapter 5)

I ask You, Father, to cleanse me totally with the Blood of Jesus, and to forgive me of all unrighteousness."

Take the time to listen to the Holy Spirit before going on to the next chapter. Allow Him to fill you afresh with His Spirit and His Love.

CHAPTER 7

GODDESS WORSHIP IN CATHOLICISM

At the present time within the Catholic Church there is a battle being fought concerning the issue of Mary worship. There is a great movement within the Catholic Church to add a doctrinal statement which teaches that Mary is Co Redemptrix with Jesus.

However, before getting into that issue, let us follow a logical progression on evidences of the worship of the Queen of Heaven within Catholicism.

Evidence of sun worship

Sun worship was prominent in Rome and along with it, the worship of the sun goddess. In AD 38 a roman emperor by the name of Caligula undertook to have a giant obelisk moved from Heliopolis in Egypt to Rome. This obelisk was the symbol of the Osiris, the sun god of Egypt. In 1585 Pope Sixtus issued a decree from the Vatican that this obelisk must be moved to the centre of the circular court in front of St. Peters. When the workmen were doing their job of erecting it, the crowds were forbidden to even speak in case they might distract them and cause the idol of Heliopolis to be shattered. When the job was finished, Pope Sixtus dedicated the idol to the cross and celebrated a mass in honor of the idol. Pope Sixtus declared that the reason for this obelisk being erected in St. Peter's square was as a sign to the world that the pagan religions had been overcome by the Church. (Published by the MIT News Office at the Massachusetts Institute of Technology, Cambridge, Massachusetts in March of 2000)

Around the idol was located the largest solar wheel on earth. It is a wheel within a wheel with eight spokes and is a common symbol of cosmic energy in paganism. The solar wheel can be seen in most of Catholic art and architecture. There is even one picture of Mary holding in her hand the symbol of solar power. Solar blazes, or disc shaped halos are placed around the heads of the statues of Mary and the saints. This is called the Nimbus.

In a best selling Catholic book entitled "The Thunder of Justice", we read this concerning what happened at Fatima:

"The Lady appeared, as the blessed mother was leaving she opened her hands, and from them rays of light extended in the direction of the sun. Gradually the sun grew pale, appeared as a sliver disk at which all could gaze directly, without shielding their eyes. Rays of multicolored light shot out from the sun in every direction; red, blue, pink, green, and every color of the spectrum. Then the sun began to spin madly on its axis and appeared like a giant wheel of fire. The sun began to dance wildly. Suddenly the sun seemed to be torn loose from its orbit. It hurtled closer and closer to earth, and looked like it was going to plummet to the earth. The people were terrified and there arose cries of repentance and appeals for mercy. Many thought it was the end of the world. Then, just a suddenly, the sun stopped plummeting downwards, and in the same swirling motion it began to climb upward until it resumed its place in the sky. The rain-soaked clothes of the people were immediately dry. This was an event reported by several newspapers of the day. Pope Paul VI, in his May 1967 encyclical entitled "Signum Magnum" identifies Our Blessed Mother at Fatima with "The Woman Clothed with the Sun", equating her directly with Revelation, Chapter 12."

In the book "More about Fatima" by J. DaCruz we read this:

"This wonderful sign in the heavens, our Lady of the Rosary of Fatima has maternally granted to the modern world in order that all may believe. She came...asking us to recite the Rosary daily and to consecrate ourselves to her Immaculate heart. The grandeur of this wonderful prodigy of Fatima will thus be in proportion to the greatness of the dangers and this sign in the heavens will indicate to us the REMEDY we are to employ against the evils that hang over us In imitation of those happy pilgrims of Fatima, let us in turn respectfully bow down before this prodigy of the sign in the heavens, this extraordinary demonstration of the existence of God. Let us meditate long on these divine facts: let us enkindle the flame of our faith in the mysterious rays of the Sun of Fatima."

At one point the current pope sent a gold rose to Fatima to honor the vision of Mary. He stated at that time that he intended to trust the entire human race to the care of the Mother of God.

The current pope has stated in his "Encyclical Letter Fides Et Ratio Of The Supreme Pontiff John Paul II To The Bishops Of The Catholic Church On The Relationship Between Faith And Reason" the following:

"There are also signs of a resurgence of fideism, which fails to recognize the importance of rational knowledge and philosophical discourse for the

understanding of faith, indeed for the very possibility of belief in God. One currently widespread symptom of this fideistic tendency is a "biblicism" which tends to make the reading and exegesis of Sacred Scripture the sole criterion of truth. In consequence, the word of God is identified with Sacred Scripture alone, thus eliminating the doctrine of the Church which the Second Vatican Council stressed quite specifically. Having recalled that the word of God is present in both Scripture and Tradition, the Constitution Dei Verbum continues emphatically: "Sacred Tradition and Sacred Scripture comprise a single sacred deposit of the word of God entrusted to the Church. Embracing this deposit and united with their pastors, the People of God remain always faithful to the teaching of the Apostles". Scripture, therefore, is not the Church's sole point of reference. (Church tradition is equal in authority to the Bible) The "supreme rule of her faith" derives from the unity which the Spirit has created between Sacred Tradition, Sacred Scripture and the Magisterium of the Church in a reciprocity which means that none of the three can survive without the others."

What the Pope is declaring here is that doctrine can be formed from Church Tradition and does not necessarily have to come from Scripture. Those within the system of Catholicism need to hear the truth. The Scriptures of the Old and New Testament are given by Divine inspiration and they alone constitute the Divine rule of Christian faith and practice. Church tradition has no place in doctrine.

In the early 1700s a proponent of the Marianist Movement by the name of Alfonsus de Liguori wrote a book entitled, "The Glories of Mary". He indicates that Mary was given rulership over one half of the kingdom of God. He goes on to say that Mary rules over the kingdom of mercy and Jesus rules over the kingdom of justice. The book goes to such an extreme that it even says that there is no salvation outside of Mary. The man who wrote the book was later canonized as a saint and declared to be a doctor of the church.

In the Catholic churches there are many statues of Mary and Patron Saints. These statues are beautiful and large. Some statues of Mary have real crowns made of gold. There are statues of Our Lady of Fatima and Our Lady of Lourdes wearing crowns. The statue of Our Lady of the Pillar in Saragossa, Spain has a crown made of 25 pounds of gold and so many diamonds that you cannot even see the gold. It has six other crowns of gold, diamonds and emeralds, 365 mantles embroidered with gold and covered with roses of diamonds and other precious stones. It has 365 necklaces made of pearls and diamonds, and six chains of gold set with diamonds. Jesus is depicted only as a little baby, a dead man on a cross, and a box of wafers.

Look at the table on the following pages. The table was put together by Mary Ann Collins, a former catholic nun. She has freely granted the permission to reprint this table.

BIBLICAL MARY	CATHOLIC MARY	THE GODDESS
Humble and obedient. Calls herself "the handmaid of the Lord."	The Pope officially gave Mary the title "Queen of Heaven" and established a feast day honoring Mary, Queen of Heaven.	Wiccans call their goddess the "Queen of Heaven".
Knew she needed a savior: "And my spirit hath rejoiced in God my Saviour." (Luke 1:47)	"Immaculate Conception" (Mary was conceived sinless, without original sin) and "All-Holy" (Mary lived a sinless life).	Goddesses don't need salvation. They make the rules.
Normal wife and mother who had other children.	"Perpetual Virginity" (Jesus' brothers and sisters are considered to be cousins).	Goddesses don't have human children.
No biblical evidence that Mary didn't die like a normal person.	"Glorious Assumption" (Mary was bodily taken up into Heaven).	Goddesses don't die.
Jesus told John to take Mary into his home and take care of her as if she was his own mother.	Catholics are the adopted children of Mary "Woman behold your son" (John 19:26) is taken to apply literally to every Catholic.	Witches are the adopted, "hidden children" of the Queen of Heaven.
Normal woman.	Sometimes pictured standing on a crescent moon, wearing a crown or with a circle of stars around her head.	Moon goddess.

BIBLICAL MARY	CATHOLIC MARY	THE GODDESS
Normal woman.	Supernatural (apparitions accompanied by miracles and healings).	Supernatural.
Points people to Jesus. Mary said, "Whatsoever he saith unto you, do it." (John 2:5)	Can make Jesus do things. A full page newspaper ad showing Mary and Jesus says, "He hasn't denied her anything in 2,000 years. What would you have her ask Him?" This is not official Catholic doctrine but it is a widespread attitude which is encouraged by pious literature.	Points to herself. Wants to be worshipped.
Knew that she needed a savior. (Luke 1:47)	Apparitions of "Mary" have promised that if people wear certain objects (such as a Scapular or Miraculous Medal) or say certain prayers then they are guaranteed to go to Heaven. The Catholic Church has not officially approved of these practices, but it has also not discouraged them.	Invoked to make supernatural things happen through witchcraft (the use of special objects and special verbal formulas).

Goddesses don't need a savior. |

In the 1993 a formal petition to have Mary officially elevated and proclaimed Co Redemptrix with Jesus was sent to the Pope. Millions of letters have been sent to the pope since, asking him to make this declaration from the Vatican. The Pope has actually complied to the point of declaring publicly on several occasions that Mary is CoRedemptrix with Jesus. However, he has stopped short of having this declared as part of the doctrine of the Church. The decision is still up in the air as of the printing of this book.

Those within the system of Catholicism need to hear the truth. Jesus said, "I am the Way, the Truth, and the Life. No man comes to the Father except by Me."

If you are currently within the Catholic Church, I am not telling you to get out. Only God can direct your steps. However, if the things that I have said in this chapter have stirred your heart, please feel free to use the prayer which I have included here.

I renounce, now and forever, all worship of Mary as a goddess. I renounce all of her names: Mother of God, Queen of Heaven, Our Lady of Guadalupe, Mother of Grace, Co Redemptrix, Protectress of Peace, Patroness of the United States, Mother Earth, Black Madonna, Primordial Mother, Mediatrix, Holy Mother, Our Lady, Mary Ever Virgin, Mother, Our Lady of the Pillar, our Lady of the Rosary of Fatima, the Woman Clothed with the Sun, Blessed Mother, Ruler of the Kingdom of Mercy, Mother of Sorrows and all other names that she is known by.

I declare that Jesus alone is my burden bearer. I declare that Jesus Christ of Nazareth is the only way to God and Heaven.

I renounce my participation in all feasts and rituals done in worship of the Queen of Heaven. I renounce the Rosary and all use of beads in prayer. I repent for my participation and ask for forgiveness in the Name of Jesus Christ of Nazareth.

I repent for calling Mary my mother. I renounce the crescent moon and the circle of stars. I renounce all apparitions of beings claiming to be Mary. I renounce the Scapular and the Miraculous Medal. I renounce the Shield of the Immaculate Conception. I renounce all medals of Mary or other saints in the Catholic Church. I declare that God alone is my fortress and my high tower. I declare that Jesus is my refuge and place of safety.

I renounce all claims that Mary is my intercessor and proclaim that Jesus sits at the right had of God, to make intercession for me.

I renounce the golden crown on all statues of Mary and catholic saints. I declare that only Jesus Christ of Nazareth is worthy to be crowned.

I repent for the bowing of my knees to these statues and the lighting candles in order to communicate with the dead. I repent for the sin of necromancy and renounce all involvement with calling on the spirits of the dead. I repent for venerating her name as the queen of heaven.

I repent for invoking her spirit and for all attempts at communication with her.

I renounce all doctrine that gives Mary any authority over my life and I declare that I will not entrust her with my life. I proclaim Jesus as the only one to whom I will give my life.

I renounce all doctrine and declarations that Mary is co-redemptrix with Jesus in matters of salvation.

I renounce all doctrine that declares Mary to have been sinless and born of an immaculate conception. I believe that the Scripture says that only Jesus lived a sinless life, and Mary needed to confess Him with her mouth and believe in Him in her heart in order to enter heaven.

I have prayed at length about whether to include this chapter in the book. Before you begin reading this material please understand that I am not a Catholic basher. There are many wonderful, truly born again believers within the Catholic Church. I personally know many Catholics who love Jesus with all of their hearts. I have seen their sincerity and integrity and I count it a privilege to regard them as friends. However, in writing about such an important subject as the battle with the Queen of Heaven, I would be accountable to God were I not to sound an alarm.

CHAPTER 8

THE QUEEN OF HEAVEN AND JEZEBEL

In the message to the seven churches Jesus says to the church at Thyatira that He does not want the spirit of Jezebel tolerated, let alone worshipped. This church was known for its good deeds and perseverance. It was a life giving church, full of faith. And yet, the church would not survive or be effective if this problem was not dealt with.

Revelation 2:18-23

18　"And to the angel of the church in Thyatira write,

These things says the Son of God, who has eyes like a flame of fire, and His feet like fine brass:

19　"I know your works, love, service, faith, and your patience; and as for your works, the last are more than the first.

20　"Nevertheless I have a few things against you, because you allow that woman Jezebel, who calls herself a prophetess, to teach and seduce My servants to commit sexual immorality and eat things sacrificed to idols.

21　"And I gave her time to repent of her sexual immorality, and she did not repent.

22　"Indeed I will cast her into a sickbed, and those who commit adultery with her into great tribulation, unless they repent of their deeds.

23　"I will kill her children with death, and all the churches shall know that I am He who searches the minds and hearts. And I will give to each one of you according to your works.

Jesus recognized how hard it would be for the Church at Thyatira to overcome this spirit so He gave the church a promise. He said that for those who overcome this spirit, He would lay no other burdens on them.

24　"Now to you I say, and to the rest in Thyatira, as many as do not have this doctrine, who have not known the depths of Satan, as they say, I will put on you no other burden.

During my years of church planting and pastoring, I have battled this spirit more than any others. I have seen it disguised by good deeds and religiosity. I have seen it disguised in offers of finance. I have seen it working through talented and anointed Christians who have opened the door to its domination. I have seen churches torn apart and saints left bleeding and wounded. I have seen pastors and leaders broken and filled with hopelessness. I have seen hundreds saints deceived and coming into agreement with it.

This spirit is responsible for more church splits than any other spirit on the earth. This spirit has caused more pastors to resign from ministry than can be counted. This spirit has torn apart many prophetic ministries.

In one particular battle with this spirit, I was nearly destroyed. I felt like running from ministry and going as far away from civilization as I could go. I was sick physically, I couldn't pray, I couldn't preach or minister, my finances had all but dried up, and I was full of despair. I felt like death would be a better alternative than what I was feeling. I began to believe that I was a dismal failure and it would be better for everyone if I just disappeared.

At this time, I decided to go away for a few days to pray and seek the Lord. I felt like He was so far from me that I wasn't sure if I would be able to break through in prayer. Just as I was about to leave town, a pastor friend put a book in my hand. She had no idea about what I was going through but she had been led by the Spirit of God. The name of this book was "The Veiled Ploy" by John Paul Jackson. (The name has since been changed to Unmasking the Jezebel Spirit) How I thank God for John Paul Jackson and the pastor that gave me the book!

When I arrived at my hotel that night, I picked up the book and began reading right away. I was unable to pray, so I thought that maybe this book would be a good diversion. I was unable to put it down. Over the next 48 hours I read, prayed, cried, and slept. As I turned the pages and read, I knew that I had not been a failure. I knew that I was not to blame. I finally realized what had happened. I had been attacked by Jezebel.

I spent another 48 hours praying and reading the Word. I repented for allowing myself to be Jezebeled. By the end of the four days I was filled once again with hope. I felt the Presence of God again and I knew that everything would work out. Jesus had given me the victory.

I have faced this spirit many times since but God has opened the eyes of my understanding to His strategy for the battle.

What does the spirit of Jezebel have to do with the Queen of Heaven?

We all know the story in Scripture of Jezebel. It bears fresh examination however, to see how it fits in with the Queen of Heaven.

Jezebel was the wife of Ahab who was king over Israel. Ahab, according to scripture, was a very wicked King.

1 Kings 16:29,30

29 Ahab son of Omri began to rule over Israel in the thirty-eighth year of King Asaís reign in Judah. He reigned in Samaria twenty-two years.

30 But Ahab did what was evil in the Lord's sight, even more than any of the kings before him.

What a testimony to be remembered by! He did more evil than any one else before him.

Of all the things that Ahab did, the thing that God was the most upset about was his marriage to Jezebel and what resulted from it.

1 Kings 16:31,32,33

31 And as though it were not enough to live like Jeroboam, he married Jezebel, the daughter of King Ethbaal of the Sidonians, and he began to worship Baal.

32 First he built a temple and an altar for Baal in Samaria.

33 Then he set up an Asherah pole. He did more to arouse the anger of the Lord, the God of Israel, than any of the other kings of Israel before him.

It was clear from the beginning that this marriage was disastrous for Ahab. Ahab was so enthralled with Jezebel that instead of her worshipping his God, Ahab began to worship those gods belonging to her tradition.

Jezebel worshipped both Baal and Asherah, or Ashteroth. The goddess Ashteroth was in fact the Queen of Heaven. It was this Queen of Heaven that both inspired and empowered Jezebel to evil.

This is the connection of the Jezebel Spirit to the Queen of Heaven. The Jezebel Spirit cannot act independently of the Queen of Heaven. The Queen of Heaven is the power behind Jezebel. It is very hard to separate the two.

Because the Queen of Heaven is so important in the operation of the Jezebel spirit, it is important to take a look at this spirit.

I would highly recommend that everyone read John Paul Jackson's book entitled "Unmasking the Jezebel Spirit", since I am not going to cover the subject entirely.

If we read through the chapters in the book of Kings, we will see certain characteristics that I want to cover here concerning Jezebel.

Jezebel was really the power behind Ahab's kingship. It was really her that ran the nation.

In one particular interaction between Jezebel and Ahab, Jezebel enters into the real estate business. Ahab is bemoaning the fact that a man by the name of Naboth has a vineyard that Ahab wants but is unwilling to sell it. He is having a major pity party and is in a real pout. Jezebel asks him what his problem is and Ahab tells her the whole sad story.

Jezebel becomes determined to get that land for Ahab, at any cost. Ruthlessly, she involved a whole community in Naboth's downfall. She had somebody else do the dirty work, but she was behind the whole thing. Naboth was stoned because of the accusation of false witnesses, and Ahab got what he wanted.

Jezebel used lies, treachery, control and fear to accomplish her goal. She even forged her husband's name to some legal documents, but she knew that Ahab wouldn't care, as long as he got what he wanted.

Jezebel also tried to get all of God's prophets killed in the land. These prophets were a bane in Jezebel's existence, because the last thing that she wanted was someone around who could see right through her. She wanted to eradicate all worship of the living God from Israel. She would go to any lengths to fulfill her wishes.

Read the accounts in I Kings for yourself. I guarantee you, you will see how wicked she was.

Today, the Jezebel spirit, empowered by and working for the Queen of Heaven, has an agenda. That agenda is to kill the prophetic, to strangle ministries, to dominate, control, kill and destroy. The enemy knows that time is short, and hates the people of God.

Some of the signs that the Jezebel spirit is in operation are as follows: (Some of these points have been taken from John Paul Jackson's book)

Lawlessness and rebellion: Persons under the influence of a Jezebel spirit absolutely hate accountability. They want to do their own thing. Often times they will disguise their rebellion with statements like, "I don't answer to man, I only answer to God". However the real truth is that they alone decide what it is that God should say.

Leaders being spoken against. Individuals under the influence of a Jezebel spirit often do not come right out and speak against a leader blatantly, although that does happen. Usually, they just tell others about little concerns, just for purposes of prayer don't you know? These individuals will just drop little hints here and there and let your own mind do the rest.

A strong personality developing a following. Most people operating under the influence of a Jezebel spirit like the limelight. (They like the limelight of attention but they hate the spotlight of truth) They usually develop a loyal following within a congregation. This gives the individual a power base from which to control an individual or a ministry.

Control is the greatest hallmark of the operation of Jezebel. Please keep in mind that there is more than one form of control. Some people have to control their surroundings because they feel like they have to hide the things that are hurting them deep down inside. They control in order to keep anyone from getting too close. Jezebellic control, on the other hand, is the type of control that no only wants to protect self, but wants to manipulate people and circumstances to get their own way. People under the influence of Jezebel react fiercely to anyone who does not give in to them.

Jezebel absolutely abhors the prophetic. She knows full well that the prophetic represents the voice of the Lord in the earth. She hates God and hates His people. A person under the influence of Jezebel will usually find a way to interrupt the prophetic flow in a church. They may try to gain control of the prophetic in a church by aspiring to become the leader of the prophetic. Once that happens, the prophetic in a house will veer off course. They may also interrupt when the prophetic is flowing by coming up with their own prophetic flow which sets itself in competition with others hearing the voice of God. I have seen services where prophetic presbytery becomes a contest to see who can dazzle the congregation more. That is a sure sign of Jezebel's activity.

False humility is another sign of Jezebel's activity.

I have found that most individuals under Jezebel's influence are very well read and up to date on the latest buzz of the Body. They believe that they have great insight into Church matters and try to use that insight as a wedge in the leadership. This is purposed to undermine the credibility of the leadership, and to eventually place themselves in that position.

Individuals operating under the influence of Jezebel do not like to be confronted. They will handle confrontation in various ways depending on the objective. Sometimes they are given to what I call crocodile tears. They will go into self pity and talk about how everybody misunderstands them. If that tactic doesn't work they will either explode with rage or give you the silent treatment, or both. One thing that I have learned is that when you think it is over, it's not! I have seen these individuals display repentance and the thing goes under ground for a season and then all of a sudden, its there again. When someone is going through healing ministry in order to deal with this spirit, it is best to not let them take any leadership role for a very long period of time. Give enough time to see if it will resurface. It sometimes takes years for these individuals to walk out their healing.

Usually if there is strife and division in a church, Jezebel is at the bottom of it. The enemy hates it when the people of God come into unity. Quite often the strife will be hard to trace to the individuals that the enemy is using. They will simply drop little suggestions into people's ears for the purposes of prayer of course. These suggestions become weed seeds of strife and they always hook in to people's wounds and soft spots.

An individual operating under the influence of a Jezebel spirit routinely draws all attention to themselves. In conversations with others, they will always draw others to focus their attention on them, whether it be by causing others to think they are great or by causing others to pity them and focus on their problems.

I would also like to briefly talk about those who are victims of Jezebel. Jezebel has a horrible effect on those who become her targets. She causes us to go into a fear and flight syndrome.

At the point that I experienced the worst attack of the Jezebel spirit in my ministry, I was nearly decimated. I felt that I was condemned by God and useless for ministry. I began to question myself. I ran off to my cave to pray, which at the time was more like going to the garden to eat worms. I understood the concept of sackcloth and ashes. You can rise above these attacks. God is in the business of setting us free and He is more than willing to do it if we will let Him.

Whether you have acted under the influence of the Jezebel spirit or been on the receiving end of the attack, you can be free! Here are some prayers which you may find helpful.

"Loving Father, Your Word says that when the enemy attacks me, I am supposed to resist the enemy and submit myself to You. I submit myself to You, Father. I proclaim that Jesus Christ of Nazareth is my Lord and that I serve none other. I resist every evil plan of the enemy to destroy my life and my destiny in You.

I renounce all involvement with the spirit of Jezebel. I renounce all involvement of my ancestors with the spirit of Jezebel.

I renounce and repent for any ways in which I have entertained rebellion in my heart. I repent for any ways in which I have refused to submit to the Godly authority that You have placed in my life.

I renounce and repent for every way in which I have attempted to manipulate or control people or circumstances to get what I wanted.

I renounce and repent for every desire in my heart to exult self. I cast down vain imaginations and every high thing that exults itself against the knowledge of Christ.

I renounce and repent for every word that I have spoken with my mouth that has resulted in undermining those in authority over me. I renounce and repent for every word that I have spoken with my mouth that resulted in strife and division in the Body of Christ.

I renounce both now and forever, the limelight of man's applause. I ask You, Holy Spirit, to shine the spotlight of Your Truth on me so that I may be transformed and conformed to the image of Christ. I ask that my life be used to point people to Jesus, and not to myself.

I renounce and repent for all bitterness and unforgiveness in my heart. I freely choose now to release all of those who have hurt me. I cancel all debts that I thought they owed me and forgive them once and for all.

I renounce and repent for treating others as less important than myself. I repent for all of the times that I engineered conversations to surround me, and unthinkingly made others feel as though their opinions and problems were less important.

I renounce and repent for false repentance and ask You Lord to give me a true spirit of Repentance.

I renounce and repent for ways in which the attack of this spirit took my focus away from You Father. I repent for allowing myself to give way to despair. I declare that You are the answer to all my needs. I declare that You alone hold my reputation. I declare that You alone are the One I serve.

Father, cleanse me afresh with the Blood of Jesus. Remove every stain that this sin has brought. In Jesus Name, amen.

CHAPTER 9

THE QUEEN OF HEAVEN AND THE SPIRIT OF COMPROMISE

Perhaps, as you have been reading this book, you feel that there has been nothing said that applies to you. What I am about to discuss in this chapter gets down to some of the meatier issues, because these are things that we can all identify with.

If you read the account in Jeremiah of God speaking to the prophet concerning the worship of the Queen of Heaven you will discover quite a dialog between Jeremiah and the people. The people involved in worshipping the Queen of Heaven baked cakes for sacrifices on the altar to the Queen of Heaven. They explain to Jeremiah that they really want to worship the true God, but every time they stop baking cakes for the Queen of Heaven, their finances dry up. They argue that they have a responsibility to feed their children and that if they do not engage in baking these cakes, they cannot feed them. They concluded that this was one of the little compromises that they have to make to live.

Beloved, the Queen of Heaven may be unable to entrap you with witchcraft or goddess worship. You may have never been involved in paganism. You may have never worshipped the Catholic Mary. However, if you entertain little compromises, you are just as guilty of partnering with the Queen of Heaven as a full blown Wiccan Witch.

God hates, abhors, and becomes angry about, the sin of compromise.

What is compromise? I looked in the dictionary and one of the meanings of compromise is to make a shameful or disreputable concession.

I have been very interested in watching events unfolding in the Middle East. There has been so much pressure on Israel to give up some of its land for the Palestinians that it is incredible. History has shown, however, that whenever Israel has made a small concession to the enemy that it was never enough.

The Palestinians continue to demand more and more, and Israel knows that.

The people in Jeremiah's day were making what they thought was a small concession. What could it hurt to bake a little cake? What harm was there in it? The harm was that God was so adamant that it stop, he told Jeremiah that he was not even to pray for the offenders, because He was not prepared to listen.

I have seen lives destroyed from little compromises. Little compromises never stay little. They take on a life of their own. You might reason that if you tell a little lie, who's going to know. Before you know it, you are making up lies to cover up a lie. It won't hurt anybody if I cheat on my tax return. Who's going to know? God is.

Do you remember Achan's sin? It wasn't as much about stealing as it was about compromise. There was so much wealth. Achan had so many needs. God had told the Israelites to utterly destroy everything in Jericho, but Achan saw it as a waste. I am sure that he reasoned in his mind that God really wouldn't mind if he took just a little bit to help his family. I am sure he reasoned out that it would help him to support his children, and wasn't he required before God to support them? So Achan took just a small amount, nothing even noticeable. But the compromise that started out so small ended, not only in Achan's death, but in the destruction of the very family he was trying to support.

I have seen marriages destroyed by compromise. A married person develops a close friendship with someone of the opposite sex and rationalizes that as long as they don't sleep together that no harm has been done. Before long they spend more and more time with the other person, and neglect their own partner. Then they think their own spouse doesn't understand them and turn to their friend for solace, thinking they are justified. I have even known pastors who have had friends of the opposite sex and they have told their wives that the other woman is their spiritual soul mate, blaming the relationship on God. It always ends the same way. Finally they end up committing adultery. The truth is, the adultery started with the first compromise.

I have seen churches destroyed by compromise. How often do pastors do things that they know are not the leading of the Lord just to keep the board happy. How many times in churches have we held on to people at any cost because we are afraid of the financial consequences of loosing them. I have seen just this scenario happen.

I knew a pastor who had a very large giver in the congregation. This individual rubbed everybody the wrong way. This individual spoke harshly with people and scared the children. One day, this individual had an argument with someone in the congregation. He went to the pastor and demanded that the person be dealt with. The pastor believed that the individual with the money was in the wrong, but instead of doing the right thing, allowed the other person to shoulder the blame. One by one, this individual had problems with others in the congregation and before long, the church was totally destroyed. The money man then went his way and left the pastor high and dry; telling the pastor that there was no use sticking around. The pastor didn't seem to be able to keep any people and this man was going to be a part of a successful ministry.

Why?

The reason is that compromise always has to be reckoned with. There will always be a consequence.

The people in Jeremiah's day compromised just a little by baking those silly cakes. But in so doing, they had come into agreement with the Queen of Heaven, and they incurred the wrath of Almighty God.

Are the little compromises, worth incurring the wrath of the Living God?

If you have been guilty of compromise you have unwittingly been partnering with the Queen of Heaven.

You can use this prayer to break agreement with the Queen of Heaven.

"Heavenly Father, I renounce all agreement with the Queen of Heaven. I repent for every area of compromise in my life. (Take the time here to be specific. Let the Holy Spirit show you the areas of compromise so that you can truly turn from them.) I turn from my sin and put it under the Blood of Christ. Please cleanse me once again and give me the awareness and the strength to stay away from compromise.

Please give me a true spirit of repentance and help me to walk uprightly in every area of life.

Thank you Lord.

In Jesus Name, Amen."

CHAPTER 10

PEACE MAKER VS. PEACEKEEPER

This chapter could really be a part of the chapter on compromise, but the importance of recognizing the difference between peace making and peace keeping is crucial, so I will deal with this subject separately.

Jesus said, "Blessed are the peacemakers, for they shall be called the children of God." He never told us to be peace keepers!

When Jeremiah was dealing with the Israelites concerning the worship of the Queen of Heaven, he became a true peacemaker. He could have said to the worshippers of the Queen of Heaven, "Oh, I understand why you are making those cakes. Yes, you are right. You have to feed your children." He could have backed down from the truth, but he knew that the only answer was to continue speaking the truth in hopes that the people would listen and repent.

There is a big difference between peace making and peace keeping. A peace maker speaks the truth in love, and keeps speaking the truth. A peace keeper sweeps the truth under the carpet so that no one is offended. A peace maker leaves nothing hidden, but recognizes that for healing to take place, a wound must be excised and the poison removed.

I was raised in a family where nothing was ever talked about openly. There were a couple of individuals in our family that could cause quite a stir. You just knew when they were in the room that if you said the wrong thing they would go off like a sky rocket. Everyone else in the family tried to be the peace keeper, especially my mother, whom I dearly loved. I remember many times when one of these individuals was particularly abusive towards me. I was only a child, but I was very easily kept quiet. I would be hurting very badly inside, but my mother would always force me to keep it all inside and say nothing. She couldn't stand a scene.

What happened in my family was that these explosive individuals kept everyone on eggshells. My mother ended up with ulcers so severe that she had to be hospitalized. My father became ill and depressed. I finally left home in my late teens, believing that no one cared about how I felt. It would be many years before God could get my attention. My mother's attempt to keep the peace took a terrible toll on all of us.

Thankfully, my parents and I were reconciled years later and God was glorified. Forgiveness and love flowed between us and I remained very close to them after that until God took them to heaven. We enjoyed many years of love and acceptance of one another.

Peace keeping destroys families. Some parents try to keep peace with their children. They give them things to try to assuage their guilt over what they believe they should have done for the children but could not. I have known mothers and fathers who have almost rewarded bad behaviour because they have been trying to keep peace. The juvenile detention centers are full of such children.

In Canada, even the laws regarding Young Offenders promote peace keeping rather than peace making. Many children are spared any consequence of their action when they commit crimes and it is proven statistically that they become repeat offenders.

Peace keeping destroys churches. When difficult situations arise in churches, many of these situations are swept under the carpet. We used phrases like, "Love covers a multitude of sins" as an excuse. What we don't realize is that when problems are swept under the carpet, sooner or later, the lumps in the carpet become mountains.

When the Apostle Paul was talking about our spiritual armor in Ephesians 6, one of the items of armor that he described was the belt of truth. He said that we are to bind our loins with the belt of truth. In Paul's day, when someone had to run long distances, they would tie their belt very tightly around their abdomen. It was known that the tighter they had the belt, the faster they would be able to run because that belt would assist their stomach muscles in their job of supporting the back of the runner.

Paul was in essence saying, "If you want to be victorious in the race, you need to tie that belt of truth very, very tight around you."

Beloved, peace keeping is really another form of compromise. As we discussed in the last chapter, compromise puts us in agreement with the Queen of Heaven.

We need to be lovers of the truth. Peace keeping never solves anything. It is the truth that sets us free! It is the truth that will set your children free. It is the truth that will set our nation free. We need to love the truth, even when the truth makes us uncomfortable.

Truth is never easy. It means change, process, and the development of our character. But without truth, we will perish.

Have you ever kept the peace? Won't you repent and ask God to help you become a peace maker?

Just pray this simple little prayer:

"Father, I love Your truth. I proclaim that it is the Truth that will set me free. I bind myself to Your Truth. I repent for every attempt that I have ever made to be a peace keeper.

Turn the spotlight of Your Love and Truth on Me now. "Search me, and know my heart. See if there be any wicked way in me."

Thank you Lord Jesus. I pray in Your Name."

Amen.

CHAPTER 11

AGREEMENT WITH HEAVEN

It is a principle in deliverance ministry that whenever a person receives deliverance, they need to fill the void that the deliverance leaves in their lives with the Holy Spirit and the study of the Word of God. It is the same principle that we must use when coming out of agreement with the Queen of Heaven. Because agreement is the issue, then in order to complete our desire to come out of agreement with the Queen of heaven, we must come into agreement with something or someone else. That someone is God!

When Jesus taught His disciples how to pray, He included as a part of their prayers the words, "Let Thy Kingdom come and let Thy will be done on earth as it is in heaven". What Jesus was really teaching His disciples is that they must come into agreement with Heaven and that means coming into agreement with God.

In order to see what is happening in heaven, we must turn to the scripture for a portrait.

Revelation 4:2 - 4

2 And instantly I was in the Spirit, and I saw a throne in heaven and someone sitting on it!

3 The one sitting on the throne was as brilliant as gemstones jasper and carnelian. And the glow of an emerald circled his throne like a rainbow.

4 Twenty-four thrones surrounded him, and twenty-four elders sat on them. They were all clothed in white and had gold crowns on their heads.

The first thing we see in this picture of heaven is twenty four elders seated around the throne of God. The elder's presence in this scripture assure us that there is an authority structure in heaven. If there is an authority structure in heaven, then we must cooperate with God's structure of authority on earth. The authority structure that God has given to His Church is the five fold ministry described in Ephesians chapter four. The apostles, prophets, pastors, teachers and evangelist were given to the Church as a gift from Jesus for the purpose of equipping the saints for the work of the ministry. The problem is, that many of the saints do not want to be in an accountable relationship with those God has placed in their lives to lead them. I realize that many people have been abused by leaders who have misused their authority. It is time to get past that. If you want to be in agreement with heaven, you must accept God's structure of authority.

Revelation 4:6,7

6   I looked and I saw a Lamb that had been killed but was now standing between the throne and the four living beings and among the twenty-four elders. He had seven horns and seven eyes, which are the seven spirits of God that are sent out into every part of the earth.

7   He stepped forward and took the scroll from the right hand of the one sitting on the throne.

8   And as he took the scroll, the four living beings and the twenty-four elders fell down before the Lamb. Each one had a harp, and they held gold bowls filled with incense the prayers of God's people!

In this picture of heaven we see that the elders had something in their hands. They held harps and bowls filled with incense. This picture very accurately portrays God's desire for His people. The harps represent worship and the bowls represent intercession. If we want to come into agreement with heaven, therefore, we must be worshippers and we must be involved in intercession.

Worship here is not just about singing a few songs. Worship is an attitude of heart and a proclamation of the Lordship of Jesus in our lives. If Jesus is not Lord of every part of our lives, then we are not true worshippers. Is Jesus Lord of your life? Is He Lord of your finances? Is He Lord of your relationships? When the elders worshipped in heaven, it was with a proclamation of the Lordship of the Lamb.

A couple of years ago, I learned about a strategy that God had given C. Peter Wagner concerning warfare against the Queen of Heaven. He was told by the Holy Spirit to gather as many Christians together as possible in the very arena where Diana of Ephesus had been proclaimed as great. I wept when I read about it because I knew that this was truly of the Lord. More than 25,000 Christians gathered and there they proclaimed the Lordship of Jesus Christ of Nazareth. They continued for many hours. We still do not know the whole effect of this on the Queen of Heaven, but a battle took place in the heavenlies that day.

The bowls which the elders held in their hands was full of the intercession of the saints. Intercession for the believer is not optional. While I realize that there are many in the Body of Christ with a specific call to intercession, we are all supposed to be involved. Several years ago, the Lord showed me the importance of intercession. One particular night, shortly after I had gone to bed, Jesus appeared in my room. I had not yet gone to sleep, so I knew that it was more than a dream. He reached out His hand to me and asked me to go with Him. He took me into a very large place. I couldn't tell if it was a room or an expanse of space. Everywhere I looked in this place there were camp fires. These fires were in various phases. Some were burning brightly, like new fires burning wood that has just been ignited. Other fires were just glowing coals.

Around each of these campfires there were figures dressed in white robes. I had a sense that they were human. These figures were tending the fires. Some were putting new fuel on the fires, but most of them were kneeling around the glowing coals, fanning the coals to keep them burning. I asked Jesus what these people were doing. He told me that these people were involved in intercession. He said the fires represented the lives of people on earth and that when the figures were blowing on the coals, that it was actually prayer that was keeping them from spiritual death.

If the prayers did not continue, the coals of the lives involved would be extinguished. I asked Jesus to leave me there so that I could help and the next thing I knew, I was back in my bedroom, wide awake and weeping. Of course, I realize that Jesus was only showing me one aspect of intercession, but I have never forgotten that visitation and it is as vivid in my mind today as the day it happened.

Another picture of heaven in scripture is found in the book of Isaiah.

Isaiah 6:1-13

1   In the year King Uzziah died, I saw the Lord. He was sitting on a lofty throne, and the train of his robe filled the Temple.

2   Hovering around him were mighty seraphim, each with six wings. With two wings they covered their faces, with two they covered their feet, and with the remaining two they flew.

3   In a great chorus they sang, "Holy, holy, holy is the Lord Almighty! The whole earth is filled with his glory!"

4   The glorious singing shook the Temple to its foundations, and the entire sanctuary was filled with smoke.

5   Then I said, "My destruction is sealed, for I am a sinful man and a member of a sinful race. Yet I have seen the King, the Lord Almighty!"

6   Then one of the seraphim flew over to the altar, and he picked up a burning coal with a pair of tongs.

7   He touched my lips with it and said, "See, this coal has touched your lips. Now your guilt is removed, and your sins are forgiven."

This picture that Isaiah saw of the Throne of God shook him to his very core. I cannot even imagine how he felt. He saw God. He saw Him face to face, seated on His Throne. He saw the One who is the Ancient of Days, matchless in splendour. He saw the living creatures around the Throne and heard them worshipping the great I AM.

In recounting this vision, the prophet Isaiah tries to describe some of the emotions he encountered at the time. He says that he realized how sinful and corrupt he was in comparison to this pure and holy God. His emotions ran from sheer awe at the presence of God, to horror at his own condition. He cried out in agony, "Woe is me, for I am undone." He expected death at any moment. He declared his wretched state to the One on the Throne and at that very moment he realized that his biggest problem was his mouth. He admitted that he was a man of unclean lips. At the point of Isaiah's greatest anguish, a loving and a Holy God dispatched an angel to take a coal from His altar and sear the lips of the prophet.

Beloved, if we are going to come into agreement with heaven, we too must have our lips seared. This is all about the words that we speak. James tells us that out of the same mouth comes both blessing and cursing. With the same mouth we sing the praises of the most High God and then the next minute we tear a brother or a sister to shreds. This should not be!

Witches, who worship the Queen of Heaven, understand the power of the spoken word. All of their spells and incantations involve the spoken word. Some witchcraft covens are so convinced of the spoken word that they speak curses onto cassette tapes. They then take the tape and unravel it so that it just looks like a bit of garbage. They then deposit this garbage at street corners or various location on roads in order to cause accidents. They will string it out behind businesses that they want to see fail. They understand the power of words.

If we use the words of our mouths to curse people, whether through gossip, slander, or ridicule, we are just as guilty of witchcraft as a member of a coven. Our words do have power and it is time to let God sanctify our tongues.

If we are coming out of agreement with the Queen of Heaven, we need to come into agreement with the God of Heaven. We need to embrace God's structure of authority. We need to be worshippers, confessing and living the Lordship of Jesus Christ. We need to be involved in intercession. We need to have our mouths sanctified.

This is a time to let the search light of the Holy Spirit probe your heart and your life. Let Him show you His grace, mercy and forgiveness today.

"Lord Jesus, I proclaim you to be the Lord of my life. I proclaim you to be Lord of my heart, my will, my emotions, my relationships, my possessions, my money, my time, and my home.

I repent for every way in which I have failed to come into agreement with you, whether in word, deed, or action.

Please cleanse me afresh today and fill me with Your Spirit. Help me to walk uprightly, in all of Your ways.

In Jesus name,

Amen.

CHAPTER 12

CONCLUSION

Rev 17:3-6

3   So he carried me away in the Spirit into the wilderness. And I saw a woman sitting on a scarlet beast which was full of names of blasphemy, having seven heads and ten horns.

4   The woman was arrayed in purple and scarlet, and adorned with gold and precious stones and pearls, having in her hand a golden cup full of abominations and the filthiness of her fornication.

5   And on her forehead a name was written: MYSTERY, BABYLON THE GREAT, THE MOTHER OF HARLOTS AND OF THE ABOMINATIONS OF THE EARTH.

6   I saw the woman, drunk with the blood of the saints and with the blood of the martyrs of Jesus. And when I saw her, I marveled with great amazement.

It is very clear from our studies that the Queen of Heaven is headed for defeat. Her defeat was sealed on the day the Jesus finished His work on the Cross of Calvary. The day that Jesus rose from the dead, this spirit knew its eternal destination. Her final defeat will take place when Jesus comes with His army clothed in resplendent white linen.

Beloved, we are not told anywhere in scripture to just sit around and do nothing until Jesus returns. Even though the final battle cannot take place until He comes, we still have a God given responsibility today. Jesus said that we are to "occupy until He comes". That means that we are to be busy, not just sitting back and waiting for Jesus to come and do it all.

Look at 2 Peter 3:11, 12

11   Since everything is to be dissolved in this way, what sort of persons ought (you) to be, conducting yourselves in holiness and devotion,

12   waiting for and hastening the coming of the day of God, because of which the heavens will be dissolved in flames and the elements melted by fire.

We have a responsibility as the people of God to participate with Him today. There are millions of souls yet to be won. There are countries and peoples that have never heard the gospel. There are people who worship the Queen of Heaven who are ensnared by her deception.

We must engage the Queen of Heaven in Battle now! However, we can do all the screaming and yelling in the world and accomplish nothing. We can bind and loose and command and demand. We will not be successful until this Principality is first disarmed. This disarming is the responsibility of every believer on the planet.

The way to win this battle, and the strategy of the Lord is Disarmament.

Be careful to be sure of the God that you serve, because you will spend eternity with whoever that is.

The message of this book must be disseminated throughout the earth. We must arise and speak the truth. I truly believe that if every believer would come out of agreement with the Queen of Heaven that her effectiveness would be severely impeded. If every believer comes into agreement with God, nothing will be able to stand in our way, absolutely nothing.

What can you do?

• Pray the prayers in this book with sincerity and encourage other to do the same.

• Pursue holiness, because the Word says that without holiness, we will not see the Lord.

• Live in obedience to the Word of God.

• Be in the Word and wrap the truth of it around yourself so tightly that it becomes the very marrow of your bones. Let the Word live in you.

• Walk in humility.

• Be quick to repent.

• Be ready to speak the truth regardless of the personal cost.

• Avoid compromise as though it were a plague.

• Love the Lord your God with all of your heart, with all of your mind, and with all of your soul.

• Get into God's awesome Presence.

• Get out of agreement with the enemy and come into agreement with heaven.

• Worship the Lord by declaration and song.

• Worship the Lord by living with Jesus as your Lord.

After you have done all of that, stand firm, set your face like flint, be resolute. The victory is assured.

I have read the back of the book and we really do win!

Bibliography

Downing, Christine

The Goddess, Mythological Images of the Feminine

New York: Crossroad, 1981

Flaum, Eric, with David Pandy

The Encyclopedia of Gods, Heroes, and legends of the Greeks and Romans

Philadelpia: Courage, 1993

Hallam, Elizabeth

Gods and Goddesses: a Treasury of Deities and Tales from World Mythology

New York: Macmillan, 1996

Henig, Martin, and King, Anthony

Pagan Gods and Shrines of the Roman Empire

Oxford: Oxford University Committee for Archaeology, 1986

Leadbetter, Ron.

Artimis, Encyclopidia Mythica:2pp. Online. Internet. 1 Nov 1999

Leeming, David, and Page, Jake

Myths of the Female Divine: Goddess

New York: Oxford University, 1994

Johnson, Buffie.

Lady of the Beasts, Ancient Images of the Goddess and Her Sacred Animals

San Francisco: Harper and Row, 1981

Nardo, Don

World History Series: Greek and Roman Mythology

San Diego: Lucent, 1998

Schmidt, Joel.

Larousse: Greek and Roman Mythology

New York: McGraw-Hill, 1965

Switzer, Ellen, and Costas

Greek Myths: Gods, Heroes and Monsters

New York: Macmillan, 1988

Usher, Kerry

Heroes, Gods, and Emperors from Roman Mythology

New York: Peter Bedrick, 1983

Dianic Paganism

http://www.-unix.oit.umss.edu/~clit387/DianaWorship.html

Artemis

http://www.noteaccess.com/APPROACHES/AGW/Artemis.htm)

Cates, Dudley F., The Rise and Fall of Nimrod

Pentland Press 1997

The spirit of Nimrod

http://www.apostolic.edu/biblestudy/files/nimrod.htm

Stassinopoulos, Arianna and Roloff Beny. The Gods of Greece. New York: Abrams. 1983.

Campbell, Joseph. The Masks of God: Creative Mythology. New York: The Viking Press, 1974.

Frazer, Sir James George. The Golden Bough: A Study in Magic and Religion, Volume II Abridged Edition. New York: Macmilian Company, 1951.

Goodrich, Norma Lorre. Ancient Myths. New York:New American Library, 1960.

Harding, M. Esther. Woman's Mysteries: Ancient and Modern. New York: Perennial Library, 1976.

Hawkes, Jacquetta. Dawn of the Gods. New York: Random House, 1968.

Hawkes, Jacquetta. The First Great Civilizations: Life in Mesopotamia, the Indus Valley, and Egypt. New York: Alfred A. Knopf, 1973.

Kramer, Samuel Noah. Cradle of Civilization. New York: Time Incorporated, 1967.

Moscati, Sabatino. Ancient Semitic Civilizations. New York: Capricorn Books, 1960.

Oppenheim, A. Leo. Ancient Mesopotamia: Portrait of a Dead Civilization. Chicago: The University of Chicago Press, 1965.

Parrider, Geoffrey, Editor. World Religions: From Ancient History to the Present. New York: Facts on File Publications, 1983.

Preston, James J., Editor. Mother Worship: Themes and Variations. Chapel Hill, North Carolina: The University of North Carolina Press, 1983.

Reinhold, Meyer. Past and Present: The Continuity of Classical Myths. Toronto, Canada: A. M. Hakkert Ltd., 1972.

The Thunder of Justice

Ted and Maureen Flynn

Maxkol Communications, Sterling, Va.

More about Fatima

DaCruz
Jackson, John Paul
Unmasking the Jezebel Spirit
Streams Publications